GRANT US PEACE

GRANT US PEACE

Rosary Meditations
for Those
Who
Mourn

BETH MAHONEY

A Holy Cross Family Ministries Book

ave maria press AmP notre dame, indiana

© 2008 by The Family Rosary, Inc.

Founded in 1865, Ave Maria Press is a ministry of the Indiana Province of Holy Cross.

www.avemariapress.com

ISBN-10 1-59471-164-X ISBN-13 978-1-59471-164-0

Cover and text design by Katherine Robinson Coleman.

Printed and bound in the United States of America.

CONTENTS

FOREWORD

Nothing is quite as consoling to a person who is grieving the loss of a loved one as the prayerful presence of family. We know that when a human life has ended, we cannot change that fact. We wonder what to say to those grieved by the loss. But perhaps it is our presence more than our words that makes the difference for those saddened by someone's death.

When a family member draws near, perhaps traveling a long distance to be with us, many happy memories come to life. The person who grieves remembers the joyful moments that family members spent with the deceased and the significance that a particular family member or close friend played in their lives together. Family ties are strong ties, and when family members gather to say good-bye to one of their own, it is appropriate that they do so together in prayer.

Servant of God Father Patrick Peyton, C.S.C., believed and taught that families can grow and be strengthened by prayer together. Yet often within families people feel intimidated by the prospect of leading each other in prayer. In response to this lack of comfort, Fr. Peyton made it his quest to teach families the Rosary.

Fr. Peyton knew that the Rosary could provide families with a simple and revered way to reflect on the ways in which the lives of the Holy Family reflected their own family life. The sharing of Jesus' family story in prayer connects families to the larger story of the family of the Church. The sharing of prayer intentions with each other opens the family to a healthy vulnerability. While our relationship with God is often thought of as a very personal aspect of our lives, in the family context it can be richly shared. We learn from our families to speak to God in prayer. We come to know from relatives that God gave us the gift of life and that one day life on this earth as we know it will end.

As Christians, we hope for life eternal, and we trust that the family itself can usher us toward our eternal destiny. How appropriate then for a family to be together in prayer at the time of a death and for the Rosary to supply the words for us to use in prayer at a time of shared loss.

This little booklet, *Grant Us Peace*, outlines a manner of family prayer most appropriate for a time of loss. After all, we are not only observing the leaving of a family member, we are celebrating the life of a loved one among us and the difference that such a life makes to us. We have known and loved a certain child of God, and this knowledge has helped us embrace life itself as a gift from God.

So now it is time to let the slow movement of the Rosary beads through our fingers remind us of the various stages of our loved one's life. They remind us of the one life we seek to imitate: that of Jesus, the Savior. We identify with the joyful, luminous, sorrowful, and glorious moments of the life of Jesus and the life of our loved one who has died. Life has its crosses and its moments of glorious hope. We are closer to God from knowing both.

Let us pray the Holy Rosary as a family, united in our relationships one to another, and relying on our God to see us through this time of crisis. God has always loved us and loves us still. Our family member or friend who has died has exemplified that love in the course of living among us. Let us imitate that quality ourselves.

May Mary, the mother of Christ and our mother too, inspire us by the way she accompanied her son, even in his dying hours. May the sadness of death give way to the joy of eternal life. And may the family given to us by God be united as it gathers to pray the Rosary at the time of death of a beloved member.

O God, grant us peace!

Rev. John Phalen, C.S.C.
President, Holy Cross Family Ministries

INTRODUCTION

Using This Booklet

Holy Cross Family Ministries is an international organization founded by Servant of God Father Patrick Peyton, C.S.C., in 1942. Father Peyton devoted his entire life to witnessing family prayer, especially the Rosary. He believed, as his motto states, "the family that prays together stays together." His witness to this belief stemmed from his childhood in Ireland and his active years in ministry when he preached in parishes and at Rosary Rallies throughout the world. His devotion to the Rosary and commitment to promoting family prayer remained a great source of strength right up to his last days in San Pedro, California. The last words heard from him before he died reveal the great devotion he had to the Blessed Mother: "Mary, my mother, my queen."

In the hour of death, many people are at a loss for words yet want to pray as a family or a group of friends for their loved one who has died. *Grant Us Peace* is designed to help the bereaved pray together and comfort one another in this time of sorrow, pain, and grief. It is equally accessible to both those who have long prayed the Rosary and those who are new to the practice. Perfect for use alongside the liturgical rites we celebrate through the *Order of Christian Funerals*, it gives members of the clergy, lay pastoral ministers, hospital chaplains, funeral directors, and all who minister with the bereaved an excellent resource to use with the bereaved or to leave with them as a comforting guide to prayer.

Grant Us Peace contains brief meditations on all the mysteries of the Rosary: the Joyful, the Luminous, the Sorrowful, and the Glorious. When using the booklet with a small group of people, you will find designated roles for a leader and for readers, following the centuries-old tradition of praying the Rosary. There are also options for scripture readings before each meditation and petitions that follow each. There are many ways you can use or adapt the prayers to assist you in praying for your loved one who has died and has gone before you marked with the sign of faith, as well as for your family who mourns the loss of someone so dear and precious in your journey in life. You may also want to include some songs to begin and/or to end the Rosary.

While the booklet is primarily intended to be a resource to assist families and friends who gather together in this time of sorrow and grief, it is also perfectly suited for individuals to use. Both groups and individuals will find it a comforting companion to the official funeral rites of the Church in the hours, days, and weeks following the death of a loved one. It is designed to be flexible, as the riches of our Catholic tradition are by no means exhausted here. When using the booklet, you may desire to add some of your favorite scripture passages or write your own intercessory prayers. Whatever you decide, we hope this booklet brings much comfort and greatly enriches the prayer life of all who use it.

How to Pray the Rosary

The Rosary is an ancient form of prayer that stems from the early Church, when monks used to gather 150 stones and place them in a leather bag. When it was time to pray, they would reach into the bag, take one stone, and pray one of the 150 Psalms. In medieval Europe, the Rosary as we know it today began to take shape as the Our Father was prayed with the stones, which were connected as beads, much like the Rosary beads we know today. In time the Hail Mary was added, and the devotion shifted from meditation on the Psalms to meditation on the life of Jesus. The traditional three sets of mysteries were set: the Joyful, the Sorrowful, and the Glorious. The Dominican Order promoted the use of the Rosary as a catechetical tool to teach the largely illiterate Catholic population the Christian story, and devotion to the Rosary became a widespread Catholic practice. The Luminous Mysteries (Mysteries of Light) were only recently introduced by Pope John Paul II in October 2002.

We hope this booklet will bring families and friends together to pray for their loved ones who have entered into the promise of eternal life, whether you have long prayed the Rosary or do so now for the first time. We pray that you will draw much comfort here. May the words of Servant of God Patrick Peyton, C.S.C., echo true throughout the world: "The family that prays together stays together."

Praying the Rosary Services Offered in This Booklet

1.   After deciding which set of mysteries you wish to pray with, take up your Rosary beads and invite others present to do so as well, if they have them. (If Rosary beads are not available, those present may simply follow along with the meditations and prayers.) Looking at the cross, we hold it while we make the Sign of the Cross and pray the Apostles' Creed, which summarizes the core beliefs we share as Catholics.

2.   Each bead on the Rosary represents a prayer we pray. On the first large bead, the one right above the cross, we pray the Our Father, the prayer Jesus taught us.

3.   On each of the following three smaller beads, we pray the Hail Mary. We then pray the Doxology, more commonly known as the Glory Be.

4.   Next, select and read aloud one or both of the scripture passages offered in this booklet.

5. On the medal connecting the beads, announce the first mystery (Joyful, Luminous, Sorrowful, or Glorious) and read the corresponding meditation provided in this booklet. We reflect on what happened to Jesus at this time and think about what it means in our lives today. We pray the Our Father.

6. We then pray one Hail Mary for each of the next ten beads. We finish the mystery by praying the Glory Be either on the last of the ten beads or on the next large bead.

7. On the next large bead, we announce the second mystery, reflect, and pray the Our Father, then ten Hail Marys, and finish again with the Glory Be. This continues through all five decades.

8. When we reach the end of the fifth decade, we may pray the Hail Holy Queen while holding the medal that connects the beads.

9. Please follow your local customs for other prayers at this point.

10. You may at this point choose to pray the Prayers of Petition offered at the end of each set of mysteries or use the General Petitions found at the end of the book. Make the Sign of the Cross to end the Rosary Service.

Rosary Services for Those Who Mourn

The Joyful Mysteries

(With Rosary in hand) all make the Sign of the Cross.

All: † In the name of the Father, and of the Son, and of the Holy Spirit. Amen.

Ldr: As we gather to pray the Rosary this day (night) for N_____, we will share in a centuries-old prayer of the Church that has been used in all parts of the world by those who share their journey of faith and who call upon our loving and gentle God to be with them.

It is not only the death of N_____ that confronts us, but that of our own journey in life, knowing that one day we too will be united with our loved ones and with God. We believe we shall see God face to face, and on that day we shall enter into the promise of eternal life.

And so we pray:

Pray the Apostles' Creed.

Ldr: I believe in God, the Father almighty,
creator of heaven and earth.
I believe in Jesus Christ, his only son, our Lord.
He was conceived by the power of the Holy Spirit
and born of the Virgin Mary.

1

He suffered under Pontius Pilate,
was crucified, died, and was buried.
He descended to the dead.
On the third day, he rose again.
He ascended into heaven,
and is seated at the right hand of the Father.
He will come again to judge the living and
the dead.

All: I believe in the Holy Spirit,
the holy catholic Church,
the communion of saints,
the forgiveness of sins,
the resurrection of the body,
and the life everlasting.
Amen.

Pray the Our Father.

Ldr: Our Father, who art in heaven,
hallowed be your name.
Your kingdom come;
your will be done on earth, as it is in heaven.

All: Give us this day our daily bread,
and forgive us our trespasses,
as we forgive those who trespass against us,
and lead us not into temptation,
but deliver us from evil.
Amen.

Pray three Hail Marys.

Ldr: Hail Mary, full of grace,
the Lord is with you!
Blessed are you among women,
and blessed is the fruit of your womb, Jesus.

All: Holy Mary, Mother of God,
pray for us sinners,
now and at the hour of our death.
Amen.

Pray the Doxology (or Glory Be).

Ldr: Glory be to the Father,
and to the Son,
and to the Holy Spirit.

All: As it was in the beginning,
is now, and ever shall be,
world without end.
Amen.

SCRIPTURE READINGS

(Choose one of the following readings, or turn to page 43 to select another.)

#1

Rdr: A reading from Psalm 27

All: I believe I shall enjoy the Lord's goodness in the land of the living.

Rdr: The Lord is my light and my salvation;
Whom do I fear?

The Lord is my life's refuge;
Of whom am I afraid?

One thing I ask of the Lord;
This I seek:
To dwell in the Lord's house
All the days of my life,
To gaze on the Lord's beauty,
To visit his temple.
Hear my voice, Lord, when I call;
Have mercy on me and answer me.
Your face, Lord, do I seek!
Do not hide your face from me.
I believe I shall enjoy the Lord's goodness
In the land of the living.
Wait for the Lord, take courage.

All: I believe I shall enjoy the Lord's goodness in the
land of the living.

#2

Rdr: A reading from the Letter of Paul to the
Philippians (1:3–11):

I give thanks to my God at every remembrance
of you, praying always with joy in my every
prayer for all of you, because of your partner-
ship for the gospel of Christ from the first day
until now. I am confident of this: that the one
who began a good work in you will continue to
complete it until the day of Christ Jesus. It is
right that I should think this way about all of

you, because I hold you in my heart. . . . For God is my witness, how I long for all of you with the affection of Christ Jesus. And this is my prayer: that your love may increase ever more and more in knowledge and every kind of perception, to discern what is of value, so that you may be pure and blameless for the day of Christ, filled with the fruit of righteousness that comes through Jesus Christ for the glory and praise of God.

THE MEDITATIONS

Ldr: The First Joyful Mystery: The Annunciation

Mary was frightened when the angel appeared to her. The angel comforted her with the words "do not be afraid. I have come with good news." Mary's response to the angel was given in great faith as she began her mission, her journey in life. Our brother (sister) began his (her) journey in life with the gift of faith that sustained N_____ in all that he (she) lived on this earth. We gather here this day (night) to pray in thanksgiving for the gift that N_____ has been for each one of us.

Pray one Our Father, ten Hail Marys, and one Glory Be.

Ldr: The Second Joyful Mystery: The Visitation
Upon hearing the news that her cousin Elizabeth was to give birth to a child, Mary left quickly to go and be with her cousin in her hour of need. As they greeted each other, the baby in

Elizabeth's womb leaped for joy, and the two women rejoiced at the new life they shared. As we pray this day (night) for N_____, we take a moment to recall all the times he (she) shared new life with us, for the times N_____ took time to visit with someone who was in need, perhaps ourselves, and how that visit generated new life.

Pray one Our Father, ten Hail Marys, and one Glory Be.

Ldr: The Third Joyful Mystery:
The Birth of Our Lord

We pause here to reflect on the birth of our Lord and on the joy Mary and Joseph experienced at the birth of Jesus. It is not an easy task being parents. There are many occasions when parents need to let go and watch their child grow and develop in this journey of life. We pray for the parents of N_____, who rejoiced at the birth of their son (daughter) and who watched him (her) grow in life. We pray for all parents whose mission is to nurture and guide the lives of the young.

Pray one Our Father, ten Hail Marys, and one Glory Be.

Ldr: The Fourth Joyful Mystery:
The Presentation of Our Lord

Mary and Joseph brought Jesus to the temple to present him to the Lord. Mary heard the words prophesized that her son would be the rise and fall of many and that a sword would pierce her heart. N_____'s parents and godparents brought him (her) to the church for the sacrament of baptism, where he (she) began his (her) journey in faith. We pray in thanksgiving for the journey in faith that N_____ walked with God and with those who shared this path of life with him (her).

Pray one Our Father, ten Hail Marys, and one Glory Be.

Ldr: The Fifth Joyful Mystery:
The Finding of Our Lord in the Temple

After a community and family gathering in the city of Jerusalem, Mary and Joseph realized that Jesus was missing. With hearts saddened and troubled, they returned to Jerusalem to find their son. When they found him engaged in conversation about the life of faith, Jesus said to them, "Didn't you know I would be about my father's business?" We gather to pray for N_____, who in his (her) lifetime experienced what it means to be about the business of the Lord. By his (her) witness, may we come to know the will of the Father in our lives and to seek out those who are lost.

Pray one Our Father, ten Hail Marys, and one Glory Be.

Option: Pray the Hail Holy Queen.

Ldr: Together let us pray,
Hail Holy Queen, Mother of Mercy,
our life, our sweetness, and our hope.

All: To you do we cry, poor banished children of
Eve.
To you do we send up our sighs,
mourning and weeping in this valley of tears.
Turn then, O most gracious advocate,
your eyes of mercy toward us,
and after this our exile,
show unto us the blessed fruit of your womb
Jesus.
O clement, O loving, O sweet Virgin Mary!

Ldr: Pray for us, O Holy Mother of God.

All: That we might be made worthy of the promises
of Christ.

PETITIONS FOR THE JOYFUL MYSTERIES

Ldr: Lord Jesus, we come before you in need of healing. We are in pain at the loss of our brother
(*sister*) N_____. We bring these intentions
before you, confident that you hear our prayer.

Rdr: Please respond: Lord, hear our prayer.

As Mary said "yes" to your plan in her life, so
too did N_____. He (she) believed in his
(her) relationship with you in life and tried his
(her) best to remain faithful to this "yes" in life.
May he (she) be united with you in heaven.
We pray to the Lord:

All: Lord, hear our prayer.

Rdr: Just as Mary went to visit Elizabeth in her hour of need, our brother (sister) N_____ gave witness to this example in his (her) own life. We pray in gratitude for the many ways N_____ gave of himself (herself) to others and for those who may have visited him (her) and cared for him (her) in his (her) illness. We pray to the Lord:

All: Lord, hear our prayer.

Rdr: Just as Mary gave birth to your Son, Jesus, N_____ respected and nurtured the life that surrounded him (her). May he (she) receive the promise of eternal life and live with you in eternity. We pray to the Lord:

All: Lord, hear our prayer.

Rdr: Just as Jesus did in the Temple, our brother (sister) N_____ gave witness by his (her) loving presence to the promises made in baptism—to share the light of Christ with others. We pray in thanksgiving for this witness of being a bearer of Christ to all those whom he (she) encountered in this earthly life. We pray to the Lord:

All: Lord, hear our prayer.

Rdr: Like Mary and Joseph when they lost Jesus in the Temple and found him doing the work of his Father, N_____ believed in the gift of reconciliation and of doing the work of the Father.

As he (she) shared your presence with us while on this earth, help us to do the same, following his (her) example. We pray to the Lord:

All: Lord, hear our prayer.

Ldr: Lord Jesus, we present these petitions before you, confident you hear our prayer. May our brother (sister) share in the eternal banquet prepared for him (her) in heaven. We ask this in your name.
Amen.

All: † In the name of the Father, and of the Son, and of the Holy Spirit. Amen.

The Luminous Mysteries

(With Rosary in hand) all make the Sign of the Cross.

All: † In the name of the Father, and of the Son, and of the Holy Spirit. Amen.

Ldr: As we gather to pray the Rosary this day (night) for N_____, we will share in a centuries-old prayer of the Church that has been used in all parts of the world by those who share their journey of faith and who call upon our loving and gentle God to be with them.

And so as we gather, it is not only the death of N_____ that confronts us, but that of our own journey in life, knowing that one day we too will be united with our loved ones and with God. We believe we shall see God face to face, and on that day we shall enter into the promise of eternal life.

And so we pray:

Pray the Apostles' Creed.

Ldr: I believe in God, the Father almighty,
creator of heaven and earth.
I believe in Jesus Christ, his only son, our Lord.
He was conceived by the power of the Holy Spirit
and born of the Virgin Mary.
He suffered under Pontius Pilate,
was crucified, died, and was buried.
He descended to the dead.
On the third day, he rose again.

He ascended into heaven,
and is seated at the right hand of the Father.

He will come again to judge the living and
the dead.

All: I believe in the Holy Spirit,
the holy catholic Church,
the communion of saints,
the forgiveness of sins,
the resurrection of the body,
and the life everlasting.
Amen.

Pray the Our Father.

Ldr: Our Father, who art in heaven,
hallowed be your name.
Your kingdom come;
your will be done on earth, as it is in heaven.

All: Give us this day our daily bread,
and forgive us our trespasses,
as we forgive those who trespass against us,
and lead us not into temptation,
but deliver us from evil.
Amen.

Pray three Hail Marys.

Ldr: Hail Mary, full of grace,
the Lord is with you!
Blessed are you among women,
and blessed is the fruit of your womb, Jesus.

All: Holy Mary, Mother of God,
pray for us sinners,
now and at the hour of our death.
Amen.

Pray the Doxology (or Glory Be).

Ldr: Glory be to the Father,
and to the Son,
and to the Holy Spirit.

All: As it was in the beginning,
is now, and ever shall be,
world without end.
Amen.

<h3 style="text-align:center">SCRIPTURE READINGS</h3>

(Choose one of the following readings, or turn to page 43 to select another.)

#1

Rdr: A reading from the Holy Gospel According to Matthew (5:1–12a):

When he saw the crowds, he went up the mountain, and after he had sat down, his disciples came to him. He began to teach them saying: "Blessed are the poor in spirit, for theirs is the kingdom of heaven.
Blessed are they who mourn, for they will be comforted.
Blessed are the meek, for they will inherit the land.

Blessed are they who hunger and thirst for righteousness, for they will be satisfied.
Blessed are the merciful, for they will be shown mercy.
Blessed are the clean of heart, for they will see God.
Blessed are the peacemakers, for they will be called children of God.
Blessed are they who are persecuted for the sake of righteousness, for theirs is the kingdom of heaven.
Blessed are you when they insult you and persecute you and utter every kind of evil against you (falsely) because of me.
Rejoice and be glad, for your reward will be great in heaven."

#2

Rdr: A reading from Psalm 23

All: Remember me in your kingdom, Lord.
The Lord is my shepherd; there is nothing I lack.
In green pastures you let me graze;
To safe waters you lead me;
You restore my strength.
You guide me along the right path
For the sake of your name.
Even when I walk through a dark valley
I fear no harm for you are at my side;

Your rod and staff
Give me courage.
You set a table before me
As my enemies watch;
You anoint my head with oil;
My cup overflows.
Only goodness and love will pursue me
All the days of my life;
I will dwell in the house of the Lord
For years to come.

All: Remember me in your kingdom, Lord.

THE MEDITATIONS

Ldr: The First Luminous Mystery: The Baptism of
Jesus in the Jordan
Jesus began his public life by being baptized in
the river Jordan by his cousin John. When Jesus
came out of the river, he saw the Spirit of God
descending upon him like a dove, and a voice
from the heavens declared, "This is my beloved
Son, with whom I am well pleased." We pray for
our sister (brother) N_____, who through
her (his) baptism was guided by the Spirit
of God.

Pray one Our Father, ten Hail Marys, and one Glory Be.

Ldr: The Second Luminous Mystery: The Wedding
Feast at Cana

The first public miracle performed by Jesus was
at the wedding in Cana. During the wedding

15

celebration, the waiters were told there was no more wine. Mary, the mother of Jesus, let Jesus know about the embarrassing problem and then told the waiters to "do whatever he tells you." Jesus told the waiters to fill six jars with water. When the headwaiter tasted the water, he was amazed to discover that it had been turned into wine. The joyful celebration could continue, and Jesus' followers began to believe in him. As we pray this day (night) for our sister (brother) N_____, who believed and trusted in the power of miracles from our Lord in her (his) life.

Pray one Our Father, ten Hail Marys, and one Glory Be.

Ldr: The Third Luminous Mystery:
The Proclamation of the Kingdom of God

Jesus preached many lessons during his earthly life and gave us examples to help us grow stronger in our belief. He spoke of forgiveness, reconciliation, healing, and service. Our sister (brother) N_____ gave witness to these examples by the many ways she (he) interacted with family members, friends, coworkers, and strangers. By the life N_____ led, she (he) experienced the lessons taught by Jesus, thus helping many around her (him) grow closer to Jesus as well.

Pray one Our Father, ten Hail Marys, and one Glory Be.

Ldr: The Fourth Luminous Mystery:
The Transfiguration

Jesus invited Peter, James, and John to go up the mountain with him. Jesus changed in appearance before them, and the apostles saw the glory of God shine through him. The voice of the Father, coming from a cloud, said, "This is my beloved Son . . . listen to him." Our sister (brother) N_____ often listened to the Son. She (he) believed in the presence of God in her (his) life.

Pray one Our Father, ten Hail Marys, and one Glory Be.

Ldr: The Fifth Luminous Mystery:
The Institution of the Eucharist

At the Last Supper, Jesus took bread and wine, blessed it, gave praise to his Father, broke it, and gave it to his friends, saying, "Do this in memory of me." Jesus gave us his body and blood to nourish us and give us for food for life. Our sister (brother) N_____ during her (his) life was nourished by the eucharist.
N_____ knew that by receiving the body and blood of Jesus, she (he) was given the strength and the courage to be faithful and honest in the journey of life.

Pray one Our Father, ten Hail Marys, and one Glory Be.

Option: Pray the Hail Holy Queen.

Ldr: Together let us pray.
Hail Holy Queen, Mother of Mercy,
our life, our sweetness, and our hope.

All: To you do we cry, poor banished children of
Eve.
To you do we send up our sighs,
mourning and weeping in this valley of tears.
Turn then, O most gracious advocate,
your eyes of mercy toward us,
and after this our exile,
show unto us the blessed fruit of your womb
Jesus.
O clement, O loving, O sweet Virgin Mary!

Ldr: Pray for us, O Holy Mother of God.

All: That we might be made worthy of the promises
of Christ.

PETITIONS FOR THE LUMINOUS MYSTERIES

Ldr: Lord Jesus, we come before you in need of forgiveness. May our prayers for our loved one
bring us comfort and consolation. We believe
that you hear our prayers, and so we pray.

Rdr: Please respond: Lord, hear our prayer.

As Jesus was baptized in the river Jordan and
began his earthly ministry, we too are called to
follow in his footsteps. In our baptism we are
called to use our gifts to assist those around us.
Our sister (brother) N_____ understood

what it is to follow in the footsteps of Jesus.
May she (he) find comfort in your loving arms.
We pray to the Lord:

All: Lord, hear our prayer.

Rdr: At the wedding feast at Cana, Jesus preformed
his first public miracle. In our lives we experience many miracles that call us to a deeper
belief in your all-powerful presence in the
world. Our sister (brother) N_____ had
moments where she (he) knew of these miracles
that brought her (him) closer to you. May we
have the opportunity to experience your power-
ful presence in our lives. We pray to the Lord:

All: Lord, hear our prayer.

Rdr: The Proclamation of the Kingdom of God calls
us to healing, reconciliation, and forgiveness.
Our sister (brother) N_____ in her (his)
lifetime gave witness to the examples revealed in
the words of our Savior. May we be a living witness to these examples as we draw closer to the
Lord. We pray to the Lord:

All: Lord, hear our prayer.

Rdr: Jesus took Peter, James, and John up the mountain and was transfigured before them. Jesus
revealed himself in glory before his friends. Our
sister (brother) N_____ lived her (his) life
focused on the presence of the Lord. May she
(he) now live in the glory of the heavenly kingdom. We pray to the Lord:

All: Lord, hear our prayer.

Rdr: At the Last Supper, Jesus gave us the gift of his life. Our sister (brother) N_____ received the bread of life during her (his) lifetime. Jesus invites us to receive this nourishment each day. May N_____ rest in the assurance that she (he) will be at the eternal table of life. We pray to the Lord:

All: Lord, hear our prayer.

Ldr: Lord Jesus, we present these petitions before you, confident that you hear our prayer. May our sister (brother) share in the eternal banquet prepared for her (him) in heaven. We ask this in your name.
Amen.

All: † In the name of the Father, and of the Son, and of the Holy Spirit. Amen.

The Sorrowful Mysteries

With Rosary in hand, all make the Sign of the Cross.

All: † In the name of the Father, and of the Son, and of the Holy Spirit. Amen.

Ldr: As we gather to pray the Rosary this day (night) for N_____, we will share in a centuries-old prayer of the Church that has been used in all parts of the world by those in sorrow who call upon our loving and gentle God to be with them.

And so as we gather, it is not only the death of N_____ that confronts us, but that of our own journey in life, knowing that one day we too will be united with our loved ones and with God. We believe we shall see God face to face, and on that day we shall enter into the promise of eternal life.

And so we pray:

Pray the Apostles' Creed.

Ldr: I believe in God, the Father almighty,
creator of heaven and earth.
I believe in Jesus Christ, his only son, our Lord.
He was conceived by the power of the
Holy Spirit
and born of the Virgin Mary.
He suffered under Pontius Pilate,
was crucified, died, and was buried.

He descended to the dead.
On the third day, he rose again.
He ascended into heaven,
and is seated at the right hand of the Father.
He will come again to judge the living and
the dead.

All: I believe in the Holy Spirit,
the holy catholic Church,
the communion of saints,
the forgiveness of sins,
the resurrection of the body,
and the life everlasting.
Amen.

Pray the Our Father.

Ldr: Our Father, who art in heaven,
hallowed be your name.
Your kingdom come;
your will be done on earth, as it is in heaven.

All: Give us this day our daily bread,
and forgive us our trespasses,
as we forgive those who trespass against us,
and lead us not into temptation,
but deliver us from evil.
Amen.

Pray three Hail Marys.

Ldr: Hail Mary, full of grace,
the Lord is with you!
Blessed are you among women,
and blessed is the fruit of your womb, Jesus.

All: Holy Mary, Mother of God,
pray for us sinners,
now and at the hour of our death.
Amen.

Pray the Doxology (or Glory Be).

Ldr: Glory be to the Father,
and to the Son,
and to the Holy Spirit.

All: As it was in the beginning,
is now, and ever shall be,
world without end.
Amen.

SCRIPTURE READING

(Choose one of the following readings, or turn to page 43 to select another.)

#1

Rdr: A reading from the Book of Wisdom (3:1–9):
The souls of the just are in the hand of God,
and no torment shall touch them.
They seemed, in the view of the foolish,
to be dead;
and their passing away was thought an affliction
and their going forth from us, utter destruction.
But they are in peace.
For if before all, indeed, they be punished,
yet is their hope full of immortality;

Chastised a little, they shall be greatly blessed,
because God tried them and found them worthy
of himself.
As gold in the furnace, he proved them,
and as sacrificial offerings he took them
to himself.
In the time of their visitation they shall shine,
and shall dart about as sparks through stubble;
They shall judge nations and rule over peoples,
and the Lord shall be their King forever.
Those who trust in him shall understand truth,
and the faithful shall abide with him in love:
Because grace and mercy are with his holy ones,
and his care is with his elect.

#2

Rdr: A reading from the holy Gospel According to
John (14:1–6):

Jesus said to his disciples:
"Do not let your hearts be troubled. You have
faith in God; have faith also in me. In my
Father's house there are many dwelling places.
If there were not, would I have told you that I
am going to prepare a place for you? And if I go
and prepare a place for you, I will come back
again and take you to myself, so that where I am
you also may be. Where (I) am going you know
the way." Thomas said to him, "Master, we do
not know where you are going; how can we
know the way?"

Jesus said to him, "I am the way and the truth and the life. No one comes to the Father except through me."

THE MEDITATIONS

Ldr: The First Sorrowful Mystery:
The Agony in the Garden

Jesus went off to the Garden of Gethsemane to pray. He took with him three of his apostles and told them to wait for him while he went into the garden and prayed. Upon his return, he found them asleep and said to Peter, "Could you not keep watch for one hour? Watch and pray that you may not undergo the test." We gather this day (night) to pray for our brother (sister) N_____, who in his (her) lifetime prayed that he (she) would stay awake with the Lord in times of uncertainty and difficulty.

Pray one Our Father, ten Hail Marys, and one Glory Be.

Ldr: The Second Sorrowful Mystery:
The Scourging at the Pillar

Jesus was beaten as he was tied to a pillar. He was helpless as the soldier whipped him. Yet he said not a word. There are times in our journey when we experience this same kind of pain when others speak falsehoods about us. Let us take a moment and reflect on the times that our brother (sister) N_____ was beaten by unkind words that others said and how he (she) remained in silence.

Pray one Our Father, ten Hail Marys, and one Glory Be.

Ldr: The Third Sorrowful Mystery:
The Crowning with Thorns

The soldiers put a crown of thorns on Jesus' head and a purple robe on his body and mocked him as king. This was a very humiliating experience for him. Through this humiliation, he held firm to who he was and did not surrender to their accusations or their mockery. We pray for N_____ that in his (her) life there were opportunities for him (her) to be challenged on principle and truth, and we pray in thanksgiving for the times that N_____ remained firm in his (her) journey in life.

Pray one Our Father, ten Hail Marys, and one Glory Be.

Ldr: The Fourth Sorrowful Mystery:
The Carrying of the Cross

Jesus walked the road to Calvary carrying the cross on his shoulders. During this walk he encountered people who gave him assistance; some volunteered, while others were forced to help him. As he lived through this painful part of his journey, Jesus accepted the help offered to him. We pray in thanksgiving for the times when N_____ was open to having others assist him (her) to carry the cross on the journey of faith he (she) walked.

Pray one Our Father, ten Hail Marys, and one Glory Be.

Ldr: The Fifth Sorrowful Mystery: The Crucifixion

Jesus was nailed to a cross and died for us. His death brought us the gift and the promise of eternal life. One of the criminals asked for forgiveness as he hung on the cross, and Jesus responded, "Today you will be with me in Paradise." We pray for N_____, who has died and has gone before us marked with the sign of faith that he (she) will be forgiven his (her) sins and will today be with Jesus in paradise.

Pray one Our Father, ten Hail Marys, and one Glory Be.

Option: Pray the Hail Holy Queen.

Ldr: Together let us pray.
Hail Holy Queen, Mother of Mercy,
our life, our sweetness, and our hope.

All: To you do we cry, poor banished children
of Eve.
To you do we send up our sighs,
mourning and weeping in this valley of tears.
Turn then, O most gracious advocate,
your eyes of mercy toward us,
and after this our exile,
show unto us the blessed fruit of your
womb Jesus.

O clement, O loving, O sweet Virgin Mary!

Ldr: Pray for us, O Holy Mother of God.

All: That we might be made worthy of the promises of Christ.

PETITIONS FOR THE SORROWFUL MYSTERIES

Ldr: God our Father, you sent your Son into this world to bring us the gift of eternal life. We come before you with our intentions, mindful that you always hear and answer our prayers.

Rdr: Please respond: Lord, hear our prayer.

Your Son, Jesus took time in the Garden of Gethsemane to pray that the cup of suffering might pass him by, but if it could not, that your will be done. Our brother (sister) N_____ followed this example and took time to pray for guidance in his (her) earthly life. May N_____ share in the promise of eternal life. We pray to the Lord:

All: Lord, hear our prayer.

Rdr: Your Son Jesus suffered an unjust punishment by being beaten at the pillar. Many people in our world today also suffer unjustly. For the times that our brother (sister) N_____ was treated unjustly in his (her) life, we ask that he (she) experience your loving and gentle embrace in the new life that he (she) lives with you. We pray to the Lord:

All: Lord, hear our prayer.

Rdr: Your Son Jesus was mocked and made to wear a crown of thorns. In this earthly life, there are times we experience the pain of mockery. Our brother (sister) N_____ encountered times in his (her) humanity when he (she) was misunderstood, and it caused much pain in his (her) life. May N_____ now experience unconditional love in his (her) life. We pray to the Lord:

All: Lord, hear our prayer.

Rdr: Your Son Jesus was given a cross to carry to his death. As we journey in life, we too are asked to take up our crosses and follow Jesus. Our brother (sister) N_____ carried his (her) cross in life, at times in silence, at other times sharing the heavy load the cross bore, yet he (she) came to understand the gift that the cross was in life. We pray in thanksgiving for the witness that N_____ gave to us in carrying his (her) cross in life. We pray to the Lord:

All: Lord, hear our prayer.

Rdr: Your Son Jesus died on the cross at Calvary. Our brother (sister) died believing he (she) would see God face to face and would share in the promise of eternal life. We pray that N_____ will receive this promise and will be raised up on the last day. We pray to the Lord:

All: Lord, hear our prayer.

Ldr: God our Father, you listen in love to the prayers of your people. Heal the pain and dispel the darkness that surrounds our lives. We ask this through our Lord Jesus Christ your Son, who lives and reigns with you and the Holy Spirit,

one God, forever and ever.
Amen.

All: † In the name of the Father, and of the Son, and
of the Holy Spirit. Amen.

The Glorious Mysteries

With Rosary in hand, all make the Sign of the Cross.

All: † In the name of the Father, and of the Son, and of the Holy Spirit. Amen.

Ldr: As we gather to pray the Rosary this day (night) for N_____, we will share in a centuries-old prayer of the Church that has been used in all parts of the world by those who share their journey of faith and who call upon our loving and gentle God to be with them.

And so as we gather, it is not only the death of N_____ that confronts us, but that of our own journey in life, knowing that one day we too will be united with our loved ones and with God. We believe we shall see God face to face, and on that day we shall enter into the promise of eternal life.

And so we pray:

Pray the Apostles' Creed.

Ldr: I believe in God, the Father almighty,
creator of heaven and earth.
I believe in Jesus Christ, his only son, our Lord.
He was conceived by the power of the
Holy Spirit
and born of the Virgin Mary.
He suffered under Pontius Pilate,
was crucified, died, and was buried.

He descended to the dead.
On the third day, he rose again.
He ascended into heaven,
and is seated at the right hand of the Father.
He will come again to judge the living and
the dead.

All: I believe in the Holy Spirit,
the holy catholic Church,
the communion of saints,
the forgiveness of sins,
the resurrection of the body,
and the life everlasting.
Amen.

Pray the Our Father.

Ldr: Our Father, who art in heaven,
hallowed be your name.
Your kingdom come;
your will be done on earth, as it is in heaven.

All: Give us this day our daily bread,
and forgive us our trespasses,
as we forgive those who trespass against us,
and lead us not into temptation,
but deliver us from evil.
Amen.

Pray three Hail Marys.

Ldr: Hail Mary, full of grace,
the Lord is with you!
Blessed are you among women,
and blessed is the fruit of your womb, Jesus.

All: Holy Mary, Mother of God,
pray for us sinners,
now and at the hour of our death.
Amen.

Pray the Doxology (or Glory Be).

Ldr: Glory be to the Father,
and to the Son,
and to the Holy Spirit.

All: As it was in the beginning,
is now, and ever shall be,
world without end.
Amen.

S C R I P T U R E   R E A D I N G

(Choose one of the following readings, or turn to page 43 to select another.)

#1

Rdr: A reading from the Book of the Prophet Isaiah
(25:6a, 7–9):

On this mountain the Lord of hosts
will provide for all peoples.
On this mountain he will destroy
the veil that veils all peoples,
the web that is woven over all nations;
he will destroy death forever.
The Lord God will wipe away
the tears from all faces;

the reproach of his people he will remove from
the whole earth;
for the Lord has spoken.
On that day it will be said:
"Behold our God, to whom we looked to
save us!
This is the Lord for whom we looked;
let us rejoice and be glad that he has saved us!"

#2

Rdr: A reading from the Book of Revelation
(21:1–5a, 6b–7)

Then I saw a new heaven and a new earth. The
former heaven and the former earth had passed
away, and the sea was no more. I also saw the
holy city, a new Jerusalem, coming down out of
heaven from God, prepared as a bride adorned
for her husband. I heard a loud voice from the
throne saying, "Behold, God's dwelling is with
the human race. He will dwell with them and
they will be his people and God himself will
always be with them (as their God). He will
wipe every tear from their eyes, and there shall
be no more death or mourning, wailing or pain,
(for) the old order has passed away."

The one who sat on the throne said, "Behold, I
make all things new. I (am) the Alpha and the
Omega, the beginning and the end. To the
thirsty I will give a gift from the spring of

life-giving water. The victor will inherit these gifts, and I shall be his God, and he will be my son."

THE MEDITATIONS

Ldr: The First Glorious Mystery: The Resurrection

On the third day after Jesus' death, his friends returned to the tomb to continue their mourning, but the tomb was empty; Jesus was not there. As he promised, he had risen from the dead. As we gather here in prayer this day (night), we too believe we will stand before an empty tomb. Our sister (brother) N_____ has died and will be raised up on the last day.

Pray one Our Father, ten Hail Marys, and one Glory Be.

Ldr: The Second Glorious Mystery:
The Ascension of Our Lord

Following his resurrection from the dead, Jesus continued to walk among his friends to give witness that he had risen as he promised. After forty days, he ascended into heaven, promising those he loved he was going to prepare an eternal place for them so that where he was, they also might someday be. We gather here this day (night) because N_____ has gone to that eternal place and, with Jesus, is now preparing a home for each one of us.

Pray one Our Father, ten Hail Marys, and one Glory Be.

Ldr: The Third Glorious Mystery: The Descent of the Holy Spirit

Those who had shared so intimately in the life of Jesus were left, after his ascension to heaven, with an emptiness that seemed to defy consolation. Jesus had promised them, "I will not leave you orphans." As we gather in the presence of N_____ this day (night), we ask that the Holy Spirit, which burned within her (his) heart, bring us consolation and strength.

Pray one Our Father, ten Hail Marys, and one Glory Be.

Ldr: The Fourth Glorious Mystery: The Assumption

Mary, the mother of Jesus, knew what it was to stand by helplessly as the one she loved suffered and died. When her son left this earth for the heavenly home, she felt as if her own heart went with him. Her only consolation was the sure faith that God would raise her up one day, to be with him—and he did. As we gather here in the presence of N_____ this day (night), we ask Mary to take the pain that is in our hearts and lift it up in the consolation of faith she knew—that we all will one day be united with Jesus, with Mary, and with our sister (brother) N_____.

Pray one Our Father, ten Hail Marys, and one Glory Be.

Ldr: The Fifth Glorious Mystery:
The Coronation of Mary

Mary's earthly life of steadfast faith was crowned with eternal happiness when, at last, she rejoined her son in heaven. The same crown of happiness awaits us as we continue our life's journey in the faith that someday we too will reach that place for which, even now, our hearts yearn. While our lives must now continue without N_____, the sure hope of a heavenly reunion and the consolation that N_____ now watches over us in the company of Jesus and Mary urge us on until the eternal crown of glory stands before our own eyes.

Pray one Our Father, ten Hail Marys, and one Glory Be.

Option: Pray the Hail Holy Queen.

Ldr: Together let us pray.
Hail Holy Queen, Mother of Mercy,
our life, our sweetness, and our hope.

All: To you do we cry, poor banished children of Eve.
To you do we send up our sighs,
mourning and weeping in this valley of tears.
Turn then, O most gracious advocate,
your eyes of mercy toward us,
and after this our exile,
show unto us the blessed fruit of your womb
Jesus.
O clement, O loving, O sweet Virgin Mary!

Ldr: Pray for us, O Holy Mother of God.

All: That we might be made worthy of the promises of Christ.

PETITIONS FOR THE GLORIOUS MYSTERIES

Ldr: Lord Jesus, we come before you with prayers for our loved one who has died. We are confident that your mother Mary intercedes for us, and so we pray:

Rdr: Please respond: Lord, hear our prayer.

Lord Jesus, three days after you died, you rose from the dead, giving us the gift of eternal life for all who hope and believe in you. Our sister (brother) N_____ has died believing in this gift of eternal life. We pray that she (he) will experience the joy of living with you for all eternity. We pray to the Lord:

All: Lord, hear our prayer.

Rdr: Lord Jesus, forty days after rising from the dead, you ascended to the Father. Your followers experienced a deep separation and pain in their hearts. Yet you assured them they would once again be with you. We are experiencing that same pain of separation from our sister (brother) N_____. May we live in the hope of once again seeing our sister (brother). We pray to the Lord:

All: Lord, hear our prayer.

Rdr: Lord Jesus, Mary was assumed into heaven to be reunited with you and with the Father. May we live a life on earth that is pleasing to you, so that we may be reunited with you and our loved ones in the promise of eternal life. We pray to the Lord:

All: Lord, hear our prayer.

Rdr: Lord Jesus, Mary was crowned queen of heaven and earth. By her example, she gives us the guidance and the strength to follow you in our journey in life. May our sister (brother) N_____ share in this glory and help us follow you ever more closely on this path of life we walk on earth. We pray to the Lord:

All: Lord, hear our prayer.

Ldr: Lord Jesus, we are mindful of your presence in our lives and the many ways in which you draw us to life with you and your Mother Mary. We are grateful for the many ways our sister (brother) N_____ gave witness to your presence in her (his) life. We pray that she (he) will be united with you and will share in the glory of eternal life. We ask this in your name.

Amen.

All: † In the name of the Father, and of the Son, and of the Holy Spirit. Amen.

GENERAL PETITIONS

Ldr: God, the almighty and everlasting Father, raised Jesus Christ from the dead; confident that he hears our prayers, we pray:

Rdr: Please respond: Lord, hear our prayer.

For our brother (sister) N_____, who in baptism was given the light of Christ, we pray in thanksgiving for the many ways he (she) shared this light with us. We pray to the Lord:

All: Lord, hear our prayer.

Rdr: For the parents of N_____, who gave him (her) life and nurtured him (her) in the ways that led him (her) to seek the goodness that lives in others, may they know the loving embrace of our Lord Jesus Christ. We pray to the Lord:

All: Lord, hear our prayer.

Rdr: For the family of N_____, who shared the ordinary and unexpected events in life, we pray that they will be healed of all pain that this loss in life brings to them. We pray to the Lord:

All: Lord, hear our prayer.

Rdr: For the friends of our brother (sister) N_____, that they may know the healing embrace our loving and gentle Father gives to his children. We pray to the Lord:

All: Lord, hear our prayer.

Rdr: For all of us gathered here in faith, that we may be consoled in our grief and find comfort in our loving and gentle God, who calls us to be bearers of hope in our journey of life. We pray to the Lord:

All: Lord, hear our prayer.

Ldr: Loving and gracious God, hear our prayers as we cry out to you in this hour of pain. Give us the graces we need to be bridge makers and carriers of your love to those we encounter in this journey of life. We ask this through your Son, Jesus Christ, who lives and reigns with you and the Holy Spirit, one God forever and ever.

All: Amen.

ADDITIONAL SCRIPTURE READINGS

Old Testament Readings

Rdr: A reading from the Book of Proverbs
(31:10–31):

When one finds a worthy wife, her value is far
beyond pearls.

Her husband, entrusting his heart to her, has an
unfailing prize.

She brings him good, and not evil, all the days of
her life.

She obtains wool and flax and makes cloth with
skillful hands.

Like merchant ships, she secures her provisions
from afar.

She rises while it is still night, and distributes
food to her household.

She picks out a field to purchase; out of her
earnings she plants a vineyard.

She is girt about with strength, and sturdy are
her arms.

She enjoys the success of her dealings; at night
her lamp is undimmed.

She puts her hands to the distaff, and her
fingers ply the spindle.

She reaches out her hands to the poor, and
extends her arms to the needy.
She fears not the snow for her household;
all her charges are doubly clothed.
She makes her own coverlets; fine linen and
purple are her clothing.
Her husband is prominent at the city gates as he
sits with the elders of the land.
She makes garments and sells them, and stocks
the merchants with belts.
She is clothed with strength and dignity, and she
laughs at the days to come.
She opens her mouth in wisdom, and on her
tongue is kindly counsel.
She watches the conduct of her household, and
eats not her food in idleness.
Her children rise up and praise her; her husband, too, extols her:
"Many are the women of proven worth, but you
have excelled them all."
Charm is deceptive and beauty fleeting; the
woman who fears the Lord is to be praised.
Give her a reward of her labors, and let her
works praise her at the city gates.

Rdr: A reading from Psalm 123

All: To you, O Lord, I lift up my eyes.
To you I raise my eyes,
To you enthroned in heaven.

Yes, like the eyes of a servant
On the hand of his master,

Like the eyes of a maid
On the hand of her mistress,
So our eyes are on the Lord our God,
Till we are shown favor.
Show us favor, Lord, show us favor,
For we have our fill of contempt.
We have our fill of insult from the insolent
Of disdain from the arrogant.

Rdr: A reading from Psalm 130:

All: I cry to you, O Lord.
Out of the depths I call to you, Lord;

Lord, hear my cry!
May your ears be attentive
To my cry for mercy.
If you, Lord, mark our sins,
Lord, who can stand?
But with you is forgiveness
And so you are revered.
I wait with longing for the Lord,
My soul waits for his word.
My soul looks for the Lord
More than sentinels for daybreak.
More than sentinels for daybreak,
Let Israel look for the Lord,
For with the Lord is kindness,
With him is full redemption,
And God will redeem Israel
From all their sins.

Gospel Readings

Rdr: A reading from the holy Gospel according to John (11:21–27):

Martha said to Jesus, "Lord, if you had been here, my brother would not have died. (But) even now I know that whatever you ask of God, God will give you." Jesus said to her, "Your brother will rise." Martha said to him, "I know he will rise, in the resurrection on the last day." Jesus told her, "I am the resurrection and the life; whoever believes in me, even if he dies, will live. Do you believe this?" She said to him, "Yes, Lord. I have come to believe that you are the Messiah, the Son of God, the one who is coming into the world."

Rdr: A reading from the holy Gospel according to Matthew (11:25–30):

At that time Jesus said in reply, "I give praise to you, Father, Lord of heaven and earth, for although you have hidden these things from the wise and the learned you have revealed them to the childlike. Yes, Father, such has been your gracious will. All things have been handed over to me by my Father. No one knows the Son except the Father, and no one knows the Father except the Son and anyone to whom the Son wishes to reveal him.

"Come to me, all you who labor and are burdened, and I will give you rest. Take my yoke upon you and learn from me, for I am meek and humble of heart; and you will find rest for yourselves. For my yoke is easy, and my burden light."

New Testament Letters

Rdr: A reading from the Second Letter of Paul to the Corinthians (5:1, 6–10):

We know that if our earthly dwelling, a tent, should be destroyed, we have a building from God, a dwelling not made with hands, eternal in heaven.

So we are always courageous, although we know that while we are at home in the body we are away from the Lord, for we walk by faith, not by sight. Yet we are courageous, and we would rather leave the body and go home to the Lord. Therefore, we aspire to please him, whether we are at home or away. For we must all appear before the judgment seat of Christ, so that each one may receive recompense, according to what one did in the body, whether good or evil.

Rdr: A reading from the Letter of Paul to the Romans (14:7–9, 10b–12):

None of us lives for oneself, and no one dies for oneself. For if we live, we live for the Lord, and if we die, we die for the Lord: so then, whether we live or die, we are the Lord's. For this is why Christ died and came to life, that he might be

Lord of both the dead and the living. For we shall all stand before the judgment seat of God; for it is written: "As I live, says the Lord, every knee shall bend before me, and every tongue shall give praise to God."

So (then) each of us shall give an account of himself (to God).

THE MISSION OF
HOLY CROSS
FAMILY MINISTRIES

In the spirit of our founder, Father Patrick Peyton, C.S.C., and under the sponsorship of the Congregation of the Holy Cross, **Holy Cross Family Ministries** serves Jesus Christ and his Church throughout the world by promoting and supporting the spiritual well-being of the family.

Faithful to Mary, the Mother of God, **Family Rosary** and **Family Rosary International** encourage family prayer, especially the Rosary.

Family Theater Productions directs its efforts to the evangelization of the culture using mass media to entertain, inspire, and educate families.

The **Father Peyton Family Institute** focuses on research and education in family life ministry and the relationship of spirituality to family.

BETH MAHONEY is Mission Director for Holy Cross Family Ministries. She has extensive experience in pastoral care, retreat work, and teaching on a wide range of family life issues. Beth has a master's degree in pastoral care and counseling from Boston College where she also did postgraduate studies in theology and canon law. A native of New Bedford, MA, Beth has authored numerous articles and is a contributing author and editor of *Pray with Me Still: Rosary Meditations and Spiritual Support for Persons with Alzheimer's, Their Caregivers, and Loved Ones* (Ave Maria Press).